The Dos & Don'ts
— of —

Web Design for Health Care

27 Tips for Finding
Patients and Building
Trust on the Web

Collin Stover

The Dos & Don'ts of Web Design for Health Care: 27 Tips for Finding Patients and Building Trust on the Web by Collin Stover

© 2015 by Collin Stover. All rights reserved.

Although every precaution has been taken to verify the accuracy of the information contained herein, the author and publisher assume no responsibility for any errors or omissions. No liability is assumed for damages that may result from the use of information contained within.

Publisher: Collin Stover
ISBN: 978-1517635503
1. Business 2. Marketing

"We worked with Collin to develop a website for our multi-location practice. Our goal was to create a website that was clean and mobile friendly, as well as something that walked the fine line between looking sophisticated enough for our younger patients and being easy to use for our older ones. Collin did all of this and more. His service was out of this world, and everything was done at an affordable price. In just the 4 months since the site went live, we've had 3,025 visits from 2,184 users, totaling 10,003 page views. An impressive 79.5% of our website traffic has come from Google, which shows that this site WORKS. We've had 45 inquiries from both new and existing patients on our site, which resulted in 24 new patient appointments for our practice. It's simple...the website Collin designed has paid for itself in just a few short months, and we couldn't be happier. What's even better is that Collin has taught our in-house staff how to run the site themselves so we can be self-sufficient, and yet he is always available to follow-through with support when we get stuck or need something else implemented. Thanks Collin!"

— **Dr. Aaron Smuckler, Renaissance Family Practice**

1. DO Read This Book (Introduction)

Technology has changed us, for better or for worse, and it is affecting the way we live, the way we work, and certainly the way that we find and interact with the organizations we choose to do business with. The health care industry is no exception. Slowly but surely, doctors have either embraced or begrudgingly accepted Electronic Health Records as the new way of doing things instead of using paper files. Prescriptions are now sent to the pharmacy digitally through the Internet, and are often ready for pick-up before the patient even arrives.

As painful as these changes can sometimes be — especially

when it seems as though not long after you think you're caught up with technology, you have to re-learn everything when things change again — they create for health care providers new and exciting ways to market themselves, find new patients, and stay in touch with existing ones.

The unfortunate fact is that some offices have been slow to adapt in the Internet age, and are stuck with either no Website at all, or a Website that is insufficient for use by the mobile devices of increasingly technology-savvy patients. After all, the generation of people who do not use the Internet are passing us by. We are entering a new era where everything is digital, and people make decisions on their care by "Googling" it, sometimes to the detriment of their physical or mental health. It has never been more important for health care providers to be on the Web.

But it's not enough to just *have* a Website. There are "buzz words" like Search Engine Optimization, keywords, Social Media Marketing, and the *Google Hammer* to worry about.

All of these things can be confusing and overwhelming. So much so that many health care providers prefer to just ignore and pretend that the world isn't changing around them. But it is.

My goal with this book is to be as non-technical as possible and to dissect the jargon that Web designers normally use. Why? Well, because I wish they would have done that for me. You see, I didn't go to school for Web design. I had a class or two in school that taught how to build Webpages, but I mostly messed around like usual in school and it wasn't there that I learned how to do any of this.

I learned how to build Websites out of *pure necessity.* I remember watching the movie The Social Network which is about how Facebook got started, and I thought it was so cool that people could put up their own Websites for the world to see and visitors would just flock to them (cash in hand).

Immediately after watching the movie I registered a Website name and bought a hosting package for like $2 a month, which later taught me the valuable lesson of "You Get What You Pay For."Anyways, I registered this domain name and I wanted to build a Website that showed videos of me performing magic since one of my businesses is a corporate entertainment company, where I perform magic and mentalism (mind reading) at corporate and non-profit events to help break the ice in networking situations.

At the time I was just getting into performing magic at events that weren't family birthday parties, and I didn't have a Website yet. I wanted people to be able to come to the site, see videos and pictures, and book me for their events.

I patiently waited for my site to be editable, which can take anywhere from 2-48 hours after you register a Website name and purchase hosting.

I was so excited to get it up and running and watch the visitors come pouring in. I had all of these design ideas and features I knew I wanted, and I knew where I wanted this and where I wanted that — I get that way when I have a new idea. Once my site was ready to be edited, I logged into a control panel, expecting to see something like the Myspace sites I had created, which definitely dates me in my 20s. I found nothing like what I was familiar with. In fact, I only ended up really, really confused. I did eventually find a drag-and-drop builder, but it wasn't user friendly at all, and I was very limited in what I could do with it. If I was going to have a site that I could be proud of that looked and behaved exactly how I wanted it to, I would either need to figure this stuff out myself or hire an expert.

I was only around 14 or 15 years old at the time, so I definitely did not have any money to hire someone.

So I got to doing some research, and I experimented a bit, and that's how I got started in Web design. Most Web designers went to school specifically to learn about design, and that is the experience they bring to the table. For the most part, they haven't been directly affected by the performance of any of the Websites they have developed. Up until a few years ago when I started designing sites for other people, I was uniquely tied to *every one of my Websites.* If they didn't bring people in, it was *my* money on the line — so I learned very quickly what worked and what didn't, which is what I am going to share with you in this book.

In regards to healthcare, I've developed Websites for some of my city's top health organizations, and my clients in the health care field enjoy over 80% of their traffic coming organically through Google, which is a fancy way of saying when people search for them, they can find them easily on the Web.

My clients' sites also have a high conversion rate of people visiting, finding the information they need, and booking a new patient appointment.

What if you aren't interested in designing a Website? What if you have lots of money and you want to just pay someone to do it? There's absolutely nothing wrong with that. While my goal is to make it a lot easier and give you some tips for designing the perfect health care Website — it often makes more sense for you to leverage your money and pay someone instead of doing it yourself. If this is the case, then you should do that. However, I still encourage you to read this book. The reason is that one of the things I'm going to be talking about are the things that Web designers do and say that confuse you, cheat you, or otherwise give you the run-around. There's lots of cryptic and technical-sounding language that they use to swindle you out of your money or make something sound harder than it really is. I remember one time sitting down with a new healthcare prospect who already had a Website but was tired of paying $600 (!) a month for Web maintenance, so they wanted to see what I could offer them to relinquish them of the chains that bound them to their current designers. The first thing they asked me when I sat down was "what do these things mean?" They didn't even know what they were paying for, and attributed this to them being "dinosaurs" or "bad with technology", but that wasn't the case.

The designers were purposefully using lingo and jargon to make what they were doing seem harder (and therefore more expensive).

Web designers use what I call "geek speak" for one of two reasons. Firstly, they're fully immersed in that language all day long, so some don't even realize they're doing it. Others are more insidious, and they do it to deliberately confuse you, like in the example above. They mistakenly believe that if people know how to do their own Website they won't hire a Web designer. That's not my philosophy. My philosophy is that there are people who have more time than money, and people who have more money than time. One group does everything themselves, and the other hires people to do things for them. There's no inherent merit to either of these, by the way. Whether you pay someone or you learn how to do it yourself is inconsequential to the goal of having a great Website that gets you new patients and builds trust with the old ones.

Personally, I feel that the more my clients know about Web design and what makes a Website successful, the better, because they're going to have a better site and they will be more informed to ask me to make smart revisions.

For your purposes, if you were planning on hiring a Web designer or you're already working with one, this book is going to help you "check their work" so to speak, so you that you can be sure that what they're doing is right, and you can make educated suggestions and have an informed discussion.

Sit back, relax, and enjoy *The Dos and Don'ts of Designing a Health Care Website.*

2. DO Resolve to Have a Website

Getting back to my earlier point, it is vital in this day and age that you have a Website. There are several reasons you *need* to be on the Internet as a health care provider:

1. Prospective patients can find you

2. Patients can book appointments

3. Young people are reluctant to call in

4. Your competition is there

5. To help people

1. Prospective Patients Can Find You
Sites like Yelp, TripAdvisor, and Angie's List exist for a reason — when people are looking for what restaurants, contractors, and yes, health care providers to patronize, they are increasingly looking to the Internet to find these things.

I recently took a trip to Tennessee and was in the Gatlinburg/ Pidgeon Forge area for the first time. I had no idea where to go, what to do, etc. What did my group and I do? We took to the Internet to find and compare. We had an amazing trip (definitely try the Alpine Slide in Gatlinburg), and we owe it all to being able to search online. This is a growing trend, and it isn't going away. While as a health care provider Yelp and TripAdvisor are less vital than if you were, say, a restaurant, you still at the bare minimum need a Website where prospective patients can find you and learn more about your practice to determine if it is a good fit for them.

2. Patients Can Book Appointments

This is my favorite one, because it means that you're making money and seeing that a Website is worth it. After just 4 months of having a Website, a Pittsburgh practice booked *40* new patient appointments from their Website — over 90% of those coming straight from people searching for them on Google. On the new patient transaction alone they made somewhere around $4,000, and that isn't even factoring in the return business they'll get from those patients coming back, or the referrals they will receive from those patients telling their friends and sending them to the Website as well.

3. Young People Are Reluctant to Call In

While it's certainly sad, it's a fact of life that people get old and they pass on. Unfortunately, some practices I have seen have forgotten this fact of the natural world (perhaps due to vastly overestimating their own powers of healing…), and they use their current patient-base as a crutch. The truth is that those patients they were leaning on to support them as "regulars" are dying and being replaced by younger, more Internet-savvy ones.

I am a millennial (boo-hiss), and I can tell you right now that in most cases I much prefer to fill out a form online and receive a response via Email where I can handle it at my own pace, and save the phone for urgencies like a sudden outbreak of poison ivy (when I am anxious to call in).

I'm not suggesting that you get rid of phone support altogether. As I said, when it's urgent, I want to call someone. But giving the *option* of finding you and contacting you on the Web in this digital age is a must.

People no longer use phones as they were once intended. People text, they Facebook, they tweet…but calling on the phone is for the most part a thing of the past. If you want to capture the younger demographic you need to embrace this change and go with it instead of resisting or ignoring (when it comes to trends, resisting or ignoring is never a good marketing strategy).

4. Your Competition is There

All of your competition may not be on the Web yet (so what better time to capitalize on that and start building your presence?), but they will be. I can guarantee it. When someone searches "doctor's office [your city]" do you want it to be your office or your competitor's office?

5. To Help People

We all get into the health care industry for different reasons, but for most there is an underlying cause: we want to help people. The health care industry, even with all of its flaws, saves lives. By putting your Website out there and sharing your mission you are able to reach more people to help them. If you truly believe that your care is the best it can be, then why *wouldn't* you want people to find you and come in for a visit? Your site being up and easy to find could be the difference between someone coming to your office and saving their life or going to a competitor and potentially being un- or under-diagnosed.

3. DO Determine Your Goals

The first step I have my clients go through when designing their sites is to determine what their goals are.

- Is this site *primarily* a way to get news and information out to current patients, or is it to try to find new ones?
- What is your primary demographic?
- How do you want people to *feel* when they come to the site?
- What do you want the site to *do* (the ability to book appointments, the ability to play video, etc.)?
- What will this site help you accomplish as a provider?

I paint as a hobby, and my instructor is always saying that you should spend *more* time planning and conceptualizing what you want to paint than you ever do actually painting. I enjoy painting fantasy scenes like perhaps a giant creature that fights off warriors in the jungle (if this is the nerdiest thing I say in a book about Web design, then I'll take it!).

So if I was going to paint this I would have to first conceptualize it: Where does it live? Okay — it lives in the jungle. Where specifically? Maybe it lives in a cave at the deepest part of the jungle and only comes out at night. So it's eyesight could either be really great, or maybe it's really bad and it compensates for that with extraordinary hearing (like bats). Maybe I decide I like the bat idea so I'm going to start with bat ears. But I want it to be more fierce than a bat because it's going to be fighting warriors to protect some kind of valuable resource in the cave. When I think of strong animals I think of bears, or lions, or even a mountain goat with big horns. So maybe my final creature would be something that looked like a mountain goat with these giant horns, but it also had the ears of a bat and powerful hind legs and claws like a bear. This isn't something I've actually drawn, but I can already start to see this thing in my head. The next step in the painting process is to do some sketches. You don't go straight to painting because you have no idea how it's really going to turn out. Just because it's in your head doesn't mean that will translate well onto the canvas. So first I make some tiny sketches of different "scenes" I could have. This allows me to quickly rule out ideas until I get one that I'm happy with.

After I've decided on my tiny "thumbnail" sketch I will start to sketch it much larger on the canvas. And only after this will I ever start to actually dip my brush in the paint. But you know what? The painting turns out infinitely better because I got that planning out of the way. Not only does the painting look "put together" because of my thumbnail sketches, but the creature looks like it *could* indeed be something that really lives in a cave at the bottom of the forest because I put in that time to conceptualize it.

I use this exact same process when designing a Website. I start by conceptualizing it. I ask the questions above and more to determine what the goals are and what we want the site to do and feel like. Then I draw "thumbails" which are just tiny sketches (on paper — not on the computer) of possible layouts and pages. Then, and only then, will I take the best sketches and turn them into an actual Website that I can put the final touches on. But the actual putting the Website onto the Internet isn't the important part. It's only made possible by the conceptualization and goal-setting steps that preceded it.

4. DO Choose an Easy to Remember Domain Name or Multiple Domain Names

Your domain name, in case you don't know, is the name of your Website. One of my domain names, for example, is collinstover.com. I also have sitesforcare.com, the20somethingentrepreneur.com, and a few others. You want to choose a domain name that explains who you are and potentially what you do. It's a good idea if you have the money to buy multiple domains, even if you're just going to direct them to the same site. For example, if you were an orthodontist office in Pittsburgh, you might want to buy PittsburghOrthodontists.com, and maybe you want to get a domain for the name of the practice, for example drbobbyortho.com. You also may want to buy the .net, .org, and any other common extension for those domains. Domains are around $10 each per year depending on who you buy them from, so investing a little bit up front so that no one can steal your name is a good idea.

It's important in this selection process to make at least one of your domains really easy to remember and spell. For example, one site I designed was for Renaissance Family Practice in

Pittsburgh. The problem is that nobody can spell Renaissance, so renaissancefamilypractice.com wasn't the perfect choice. What they decided to do was buy renaissancefamilypractice.com to save their name and keep anyone else from using it, and then also buy rfpcares.com where they would send everybody since it's a lot easier to remember and spell.

To check if a domain name is available for purchase, Google "Domain Availability" and click on one of the links. I like instantdomainsearch.com the most because it gives you instant availability results and the ability to purchase as you type.

It's often that a domain name you really, really love won't be available for purchase. This happens for a few potential reasons. The first is that the site is already in use by a legitimate business. In this case, you may want to rethink the direction you're taking the domain name picking anyways, because you don't want people to go to this other site mistakenly.

The other reason a domain may not be available is because there are "Reseller Businesses" whose business model consists of buying domain names that they think other people would like to have and then selling them to those people for a huge profit.

In fact the most expensive domain ever resold was CarInsurance. com, and it sold for a whopping $49,700,000! There is one course of action that you can take, though, if you *really* need a domain that isn't available. Google this phrase: WHOIS lookup. Click on one of the top results and put in the domain name you're looking for. It will look into the Internet registry and give you information on who owns the domain and how you can contact them. Sometimes this contact information is private and it only gives you the name and Email of where they purchased their domain name, but other times you can get the direct contact information for the person who owns the site. If the name is really important to you, you can offer to buy it from that person by Emailing or calling them. This doesn't mean they have to accept of course or that it will be cheap, but it may be worth a shot.

Another thing you should look for in the WHOIS lookup is the expiration date. Sometimes people let their domain names expire and then they can be snatched up. I did this myself when I bought the20somethingentrepreneur.com. What I really wanted was 20somethingentrepreneur.com, without the "the", but it was already taken. I checked the expiration date, and it was only in a couple weeks. Once it expired I came in and bought it for $10 and now I own it.

5. DON'T Pay a Fortune for Hosting

When I say hosting I am referring to the company that keeps your Website on the Internet. Your Website has to actually physically live on computers that your visitors connect to — that's how the Internet works. Hosting companies sell you space on their computers, as well as a myriad of additional services.

Unfortunately, I have seen too often in the health care field, Web design companies that will quote hundreds of dollars a month for hosting. My philosophy is that you don't *need* to go through your Web design company for hosting. For all of my clients I help them set up a hosting account with an online company and I help manage that, but I don't personally host any of their Websites (why would I? There are plenty of companies who are big enough that they can do it cheaper than I can).

The reality is that hosting is cheap. For a local health care site, you can get away with paying around $10/month. This is because the purpose of a health care site is to give people information, book an appointment, and that is it. You aren't creating a new Facebook or Twitter where you'll have millions of visitors on at once that necessitate buying hundreds of computers for your

Website to live on. Sadly, many Web design companies take

advantage of health care providers' lack of knowledge of how the

Internet really works, and charge hundreds of dollars a month for

what could just as well cost the provider $10.

6. DO Develop a Layout Plan Before Actually Starting the Design Work

I talked about this earlier with my painting example, but I'll go into a little more detail as far as what I specifically ask my clients to do. First is the conceptualization phase, where you ask the questions from Tip #3. Next I ask my clients to come up with a page hierarchy. In other words, I want to know what pages will be on the site, which pages will be the most important, and what pages will be in the top navigation menu of the Website. I may agree with them or disagree at this point as far as what pages should be important (more on that in the next two tips), but we can at least figure out all the pages they want and get a general idea of what they want the Website to do.

At this point I will pull out pen and paper and sketch out possible layouts based on their goals and the feeling they want the site to give the visitor. This is both an art and a science, and it improves with practice. I will usually, right at our initial brainstorming meeting, draw out the layouts of the primary pages (Example below). The client will then look at my sketches and make suggestions in real-time so that I can modify what's on the paper. Once we have approved sketches I'll translate that into a sample page on the Internet with dummy content. Most times they love it — other times the page didn't translate well from how it looked on paper to how it looks now that it's a live Web page, so we make more changes. I like to make revisions as I go versus most who make a couple of "free rounds of revisions" once the Website is finished. I think it makes more sense to work with the client the whole time sharing my work and getting feedback as we go along instead of designing the whole Website and then redesigning the whole Website if it doesn't look how the client expected it to. This saves us both a lot of disappointment (and money).

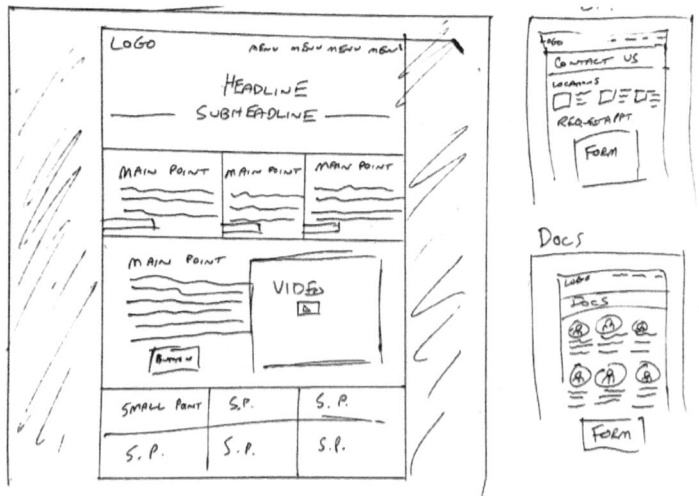

Getting the designs right on paper before you even log on to the computer is a great

first step

7. DON'T Make the Site Complicated or Cluttered

The goal of a Website is to help visitors get where they need to be — anything beyond this one goal is superfluous and should be avoided at all costs. The easiest place to clutter your Website is in the main navigation at the top of every page. The tendency of those who don't know any better is to link to *every single page* in that top navigation, when in reality there are only about 4 or 5 pages you need to link to (which I will detail in the next tip).

Take a look at this Dallas-based orthopedic site that I did not develop. There are 9 links in the header area, and then when you hover over some of those links they reveal even more links, and those to even more! This brings the grand total number of links to 38(!). Do you really think it should take 38 pages to tell a potential patient what you do, what makes you different, and why they should call you right now? Remember: the number one focus of your Website is to give visitors the information they need and get them to book an appointment as soon as possible. For my clients the average number of pages visited in a session for each visitor is around 2.5. Is this because their site sucks and people want to leave? Of course not — it's because we have designed the

Website in such a way that it gets people the information they

need and gets them to book an appointment as soon as humanly

possible.

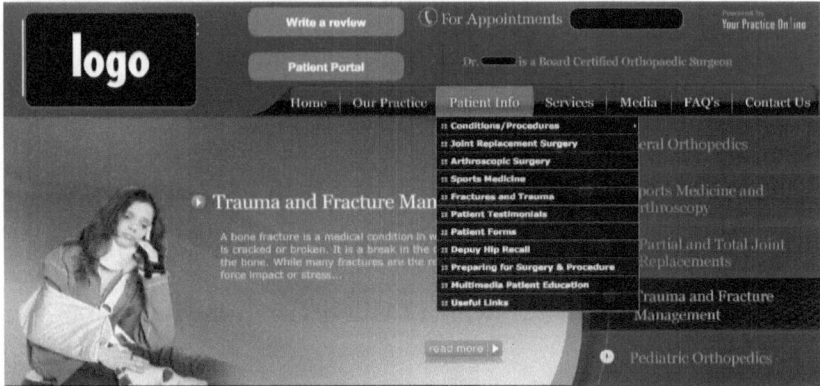

38 pages in the navigation is about 33 pages too many.

**Take a look at the pages that Website lists in their top
navigation:**

- Home
- Our Practice (Which opens a drawer with the following
when you hover over it:)
    - Dr. U
    - Dr. J
    - Dr. C
    - Physician Assistant
    - Physical Therapist
    - Practice Administrator
    - Staff
    - Our Philosophy
    - Photo Gallery
    - Practice Locations
    - Contact Us

- Patient Info (Which opens a drawer with the following:)
    - Conditions/Procedures
        * Hips
        * Knees
        * Shoulders
        * Foot & Ankle
    - Joint Replacement Surgery
    - Arthroscopic Surgery
    - Sports Medicine
    - Fractures and Trauma
    - Patient Testimonials
    - Patient Forms
    - Depuy Hip Recall
    - Preparing for Surgery & Procedure
    - Multimedia Patient Education
    - Useful Links
- Services
- Media
- FAQ's
- Contact Us (again)

Now I want you to put yourself in the shoes of a potential
new patient. You've just been diagnosed with some kind of bone
disorder by your general practitioner and you're sent to this
Website. You're scared, you're nervous, and you want answers on
how to fix your problems. Do you have *any idea* where you should
go first? There are so many unnecessary pages in this navigation.
The ones that stick out are: All of the staff pages (why do these
need to be in the top navigation? Even if you wanted a page that
described all of the staff, couldn't you put them all on a single

page instead of linking to them individually?), Photo Gallery
(why the heck do I need to go to a single page, or why would I
want to, see photos? Couldn't the photos be around the site as
supplement to the copy, or text, on the pages?), and all of the
conditions pages (again, why can't these be linked to on a single
page?).

Enough ripping this site to shreds (they make it too easy) —
it's time to explain my philosophy when it comes to navigation on
a Website and how to do it the *right* way.

8. DO Include the Main 5 Pages: Home, About, Where to Start, T&C, Blog

These are not just the only pages you need in your navigation, but the only pages you need on your Website, *in general.* Naturally we end up including a few more pages based on a provider's needs and goals, but you can have a generally great Website with just these 5 pages.

Here's what each of these pages does for your site:

Home: This is the first page that potential patients will see when visiting your site, so its whole goal is to pull them in and take them to a page where they can book an appointment or give you their contact information (which we will talk about in the tip, *DO Give a Lead Generator*).

The subtle details of the homepage will change depending on the Website, but the elements should be pretty much the same all-around. Take a look at one of my sites, collinstover.com, for an example. The first thing you see on the page is a welcome video from me, because people who are hiring a magician (my other job) are often looking for some kind of video of a performance, and because my personality is such a large part of my business and marketing. I wanted to put that personality at the forefront. I don't auto-play the video because most visitors find it annoying and will just click off if they can't quickly find the volume or pause button. Don't expect everyone to know that you can just click anywhere on the video to stop it.

Below that I give a headline that explains what I do, and below that I have some recommended links that first-time visitors should click. It's clean, and all of the important information is above the fold, which means that visitors don't have to scroll to get the good stuff.

The most important elements on your homepage are a headline that explains the problem you solve, a way to capture leads, preferably by giving something away for free in exchange for a visitor's contact information (again, *DO Give a Lead Generator*), and links that guide new visitors to where they need to be.

By the way, when I say to have a headline, I mean a headline that is about a sentence or two long that is *benefit-driven.* This is *not* a tag-line or slogan. It is a headline that explains the problems you solve and why your visitor should stay on your site.

About: Most treat the about page as a place to just give a history lesson on the organization. For example, a doctor's office might say, "ABC Family Practice was founded in 1955 and has been a staple in the XYZ community for over 60 years." and blah blah blah. I hate to be blunt, but no one cares about that, and no one cares about your history lesson either. People care about "What's in it for me?"

Instead, that office should focus on what their demographic cares about most. Maybe community *is* important to their patients, so a statement explaining how long they've been around serving the community might be a good idea, but I doubt it's the *first* thing their patients care about, so they could have a stronger start.

A better start to the "About" page might go something like this: "ABC Family Practice is committed to keeping you healthy and delivering the absolute best in compassionate and dignified care. We've been a staple in this community for over 60 years, and from the beginning we have put all of the emphasis on treating you, our patient, like family. We strive to be different in a country full of doctor's offices that treat you more like a bank than a neighbor."

That's a much better start, because it focuses on the patient, *not* the doctor's office (more on this in the next tip).

The other important element on an "about" page is a call to action or next step. This next step may be booking an appointment, or giving an Email in exchange for a free report, or taking a quiz. Just don't leave them hanging at the end of the "About" page with nothing to do, because they may just decide to leave. Hopefully you've gotten them excited and warm 'n' fuzzy with your "about" copy, so now it's time to capitalize on that. I would recommend that if you aren't an experienced copywriter that you hire someone to do that for you. If you need a recommendation, just let me know and I will introduce you to my copywriter.

Where to Start: This can be called "Where to Start," "What to Do Next," "Start Here," or any number of things, but it's on this page that you want to set expectations and give your potential patients options for how to proceed. For example, on my "What Happens Next" page on my magician site, I explain that what I would like to do is schedule an appointment with them so that we can talk about their event and determine if magician services are right for them. I frame it in a way that sounds like I'm doing this just for them, when, in reality, it's more about me leaving a positive impression by being different and meeting them instead of just Emailing back and forth. It also allows me to do my selling in-person, which I'm better at than I am over Email or phone (there's a free bonus tip).

Once they fill out that contact form they're taken to a thank-you page with a video that *does* autoplay. This page is meant to stop them in their tracks so they listen to my voice. I'm going to further reinforce what they should expect: I'm going to Email them with my date availability, and we're going to schedule a day to meet in person before we are able to work together. I implemented this video because I can't tell you how many people went through my "what happens next" page, completely ignored the "meeting" part, and were confused when I told them that I require a meeting up-front before any booking can be made. The thank-you page with the video gives them another opportunity to learn what to expect, as does the automated Email they receive after filling out the form (more on automation later).

The number one way to ensure perfect customer service is to manage expectations. That's all it is. if you went to a random restaurant and asked for free food, you wouldn't be surprised if they didn't give it to you. But if a restaurant advertised that they had free food every Wednesday and you expected that to be true, you would call it horrible customer service if you went in on Wednesday and had to pay for your meal. The same goes for every business. If you can use your site to manage expectations through this extremely important "what happens next" page and the subsequent thank you page, I guarantee you will have happier customers.

Terms and Conditions/Privacy Policy: Honestly, this is just legalese to protect your butt. You can have a lawyer draft one and spend tons of money, or you can go to my site, find the terms of use in the footer, and copy it, modifying it for your use as needed. I did the same thing. Just know that I am not a lawyer and take no legal responsibility, implied or otherwise, for any page on your Website.

Blog: We're going to talk about your blog in another part of this book, but I will tell you right now that if you want to be found on Google by people who aren't actively searching for you specifically (maybe they're searching for your competition), then blogging needs to be a priority.

That's it! Quite honestly, you can have a close to perfect site with just those 5 pages. What more do your patients truthfully need to make a decision? The "what to do next" page can double as your contact page if you like, or you can create a 6th: Contact Us, which also lists your locations. There is absolutely no reason to have 38 pages in your navigation like the previous example.

9. DO Focus on the Patient, Not on Your Practice

When it comes to building a Website and especially to writing the copy (text) on said site, focusing on the *patient* and *what's in it for them* is the single most important thing you can do. If you only read this tip you would fix about 90% of the other "DON'TS" I give you, because they are, very often, the practice being self-serving.

For example, do you *really* need a separate page on your Website for every doc, PA, EA, AA, or XYZ? No. These are pages that we create to make ourselves and the people on our teams feel good. However, I would recommend putting only the most vital of people to your brand (ask yourself: who is the *face* of this office?) at the forefront, and even then I would recommend perhaps just a section on the "about" page instead of creating a whole separate page for each of these people.

If you want to make people feel good, you can just put a photo of the whole office together on the "about" page to make it warm 'n' fuzzy. But a separate about page for every person on-staff is a bit much. For each page that you are looking to create, ask

34

yourself, does this:

- (A) give the patient information vital to them working with us in the way that we want them to work with us, and

- (B) move the patient along to booking an appointment or giving us their information so we can follow up with them?

If the answer to *either* of those questions for any given page or element is *no* or *not really* then it shouldn't be done. These are the two goals of your Website.

10. DO Use a Content Management System

Shhhh…this is a secret. This is how Web designers create "fully custom" sites without taking months and months and months to develop them.

What is a Content Management System? A CMS is basically a Website builder. It's a way of managing your Website and the pages or blog posts on it along with any pictures, video, files, etc. in a user-friendly way. In order to fully appreciate what this means, I need to give you a brief history lesson.

Back in the dawn of personal computing, when the late Steve Jobs was just getting started with Apple and computers were just giant calculators for hobbyist geeks and hackers, which used to be a good term, there was no such thing as a user interface. The only way to do anything on a computer was to use punch cards, which if you used a computer in the early 80's you may remember. It wasn't until the early 1970's that the GUI, or Graphic User Interface, was created. This opened up a whole new world of personal computing, and helped bridge the gap between hobbyists and everyday people. Apple products like the early Lisa and

Macintosh used a mouse and keyboard, and you could actually see a desktop, which was revolutionary.

Soon, computers evolved and became more and more user friendly — more and more intuitive to use. Today, we carry computers everywhere, in our pockets.

Hopefully I didn't bore you with that history lesson, but I gave it for an important reason.

I want you to think of the Content Management System as that Graphical User Interface that bridged the gap between the geeks and the everyday man. Before the CMS, you had to manually type in pages and pages of code to build a Website. If you got something wrong, your site wouldn't work and you would have to go through all of the code to find your mistake. With a CMS, your starting point is already a functional, albeit generic, Website. This means that you're a lot closer to getting what you want than if you started from scratch. It's almost like making cookies. You could grow every single ingredient yourself, get the eggs from chickens that you raise in your backyard, and bake them that way. Or, you could go to the store, buy all of the same ingredients for less than you would spend to create your

mini-farm, and get the same result. When you start with the
ingredients already there, you're able to make things a lot faster
than if you made them from scratch. This is the essence of the
CMS. You start with a basic site that the CMS generates, and
then all you have to do is find a theme you like, easily install it,
and modify from there.

This is *exactly* what I would say about 95% of Web designers
today do. I don't have the exact statistics, but I can tell you that
the vast majority aren't tirelessly coding an entire Website from
scratch, even if they say it is completely custom. They're installing
a CMS, finding a theme that's as close to what you want as
possible, and then editing that theme to give you what you want.
Many of them don't even tell you this is what they're doing,
although I always do.

Let me be clear: there's nothing wrong with using a CMS.
That would be akin to saying that it's wrong to use a mouse and
keyboard and that you should be using punch cards. Or that it's
wrong to buy things at the store, and you should be required to
grow everything in your backyard. Anything that makes life easier
is an advancement of our race. But you *should* know that this

is what they are doing, versus painstakingly hand-coding every Website as if they were in the 90's or early 2000's.

There are a number of CMSs out there, the leader and my personal favorite being Wordpress, and get this: most of them, including Wordpress, are *free*.

This doesn't necessarily mean that designing a site is *easy*. It still takes a specialized skill set that it took me several years to master, but there is no arguing that it's easier to complete a Website now than it was in the 90's or early 2000's.

What I love about a CMS is that once I set it up and design the site around it, it's really easy for your staff to create blogs and modify pages by themselves. This way I can work on (and bill you for) more important things like actually changing the functionality on your site, while you can easily put up new content yourself if you so choose.

11. DO Care About SEO (Search Engine Optimization)...

As I said, an average of 80% of my clients' Website traffic comes organically from Google, meaning that when people search for them, they *find* them. This means that on some level, their SEO is working. There are certain things they could be doing to get onto Google *more* when people search for competitors or general terms like "doctor Pittsburgh," but I can't force them to do those things (mainly blogging, which I'll talk about in tip #13). The great thing about SEO is that it gets you *new* patients that may have never heard of you or your practice before. Ideally, when someone searches for information in your niche, you want your Website to pop up. If you're a cancer center in Pittsburgh, you want to rank for "Cancer Treatment Pittsburgh." In a perfect world, you would also rank for more general searches like "I've just been diagnosed with cancer, what do I do?", but there's a reason I recommend that my clients don't focus on ranking for general searches like that, which I describe next.

12. ...But DON'T Focus On It Too Much

Being at the top spot on the top page of Google for your keywords will certainly get you lots of new patients, but just know that it is a *constantly* moving target, and that you could spend a lot of time and a lot of money working on it. This is why I recommend that instead of putting a lot of time, effort, and money into developing the perfect SEO strategy that gets you to the top page every time, that you take some of the tips I will give you for SEO and combine them with more traditional forms of marketing, and spend the rest of your time focusing on innovating your business and taking care of your current customers so that they in turn refer you to new people.

Because the world of Search Engine Optimization is a magical place. If you can put the time and money into it you are definitely going to get a lot of visitors to your site, but there comes a point where you start to see diminishing returns.

One of the main things that I don't like about the way that most present Search Engine Optimization is that it really is only *half* of the equation. SEO is how you get people to your site, but unless you're making all of your money off of ad placement on your Website (which most health care sites do *not*), just getting people there isn't enough. You need to get them to take some action.

This is where what we call "Direct Response Marketing" comes in. This is how we increase the number of people who come to our site and actually book an appointment, or actually fill out a form to talk to you, or whatever it is that you want them to do. We'll talk about this in the tip I keep mentioning, *DO Give a Lead Generator.*

Web site traffic is a numbers game, but it may not be the numbers you think. For example, would you rather get 1000 people to your site each day with your SEO strategy and only convert 10 of them, or would you rather get 100 people to your site each day and convert 20 of them? Obviously it makes more sense to focus on getting the people who *are* visiting your site to book an appointment than it does to just bring more non-paying visitors to your site. This shift in mentality alone can completely change the results you receive from your Website.

13. DO Blog

This is where I always get the most resistance, and I
completely understand why. Most people want a Website that
they can simply set up and forget about. We have this vision of
setting up a site and then just passively watching as visitors storm
the gates. I had the same vision when I got started designing sites
around age 15. The truth is, just *having* a Website is the minimum
ante to play. It takes more than that to get potential patients
to find you and *visit* the site. Most try to mystify SEO (Search
Engine Optimization) like it's some kind of magical trick that
you do once and see results immediately. The truth is that when it
comes to search engines like Google, no matter how many times
a year their "algorithms" change, they're looking for three things
when displaying search results to a visitor:

1. Relevant Content

2. New Content

3. Popular Content

Ignoring the third (because let's face it, your health care site
will *most likely* never be as popular as Buzzfeed, Facebook, Twitter,

or even Web MD, unless that's your goal. In which case go for it, but don't ask me how to do it, because I have *no idea*), look at the first two: *relevant* and *new*.

When somebody searches for "Heart Condition Pittsburgh," Google is going to look for content that has those keywords in it in a way that it believes is most relevant to the searcher. But it also doesn't want to give you out-dated information, so it's going to look for sites that are consistently updating their Website. These will be among the top search results, along with sites that also have the popular factor going for them, like the local CBS station.

The way *you* can get to the top of these lists is through blogging. It is *not* as difficult as it sounds, and you can always hire someone to do it for you if need be.

Blogging is the number one thing that I recommend that every single one of my clients do, and it also gets lots of push-back and lots of questions. Here are some answers to the most common.

Q: How Do I Come Up With Topics?

A: Sit down with your entire staff for about 20 minutes with a pad of paper in hand. Ask them what the most common questions they receive from patients are. You should come up with 7-8 really easily. Getting to 10 will be harder. The goal is to get to around 20. Don't skip over any questions for being "dumb" — this will discourage others from coming up with ideas. Write everything down. By the end I want you to narrow it down to 12-16 of the most common questions you receive from patients. Then, every week, I want you to interview someone, or multiple people, who have the answer. Transcribe those answers, and those are the blogs. Rinse and repeat.

Q: How Often Should I Blog?

A: That's up to you. For optimal results I recommend blogging once a week. This is often enough that you should see a boost in search engine traffic in a relatively short period of time, but not so often that you fail to do it from getting "burnt out."

I also highly recommend setting a precise time each week to do your blogging. Pick a less-than-busy time that you'll be the least likely to get disturbed or want to procrastinate. Then buckle down and get it up on the site.

Q: How Long Should Blogs Be?

A: This is entirely up to you. I've written blogs that are a couple sentences, and I've written blogs that are thousands of words long. The best answer to any "how long" question is, "as long as it needs to be to get your point across."

Q: HOW Do I Blog? Like, technically speaking.

A: This is something I teach all of my clients how to do in a training session, but it's pretty intuitive if you've ever posted to Facebook before. This is why we are using a CMS (Content Management System — See Tip #10) like Wordpress that makes it really easy to post blogs with the click of a few buttons. No need to do any kind of "coding" that will just serve to make you not want to blog.

Q: Can I Just <u>Not</u> Blog?

A: Sure, you can. But you will likely *only* get visitors to your site who are actively searching for your name (i.e. have heard of you before). So while you'll still get appointments through the site, most of them are going to be from people who would have called you anyways.

I get that you're busy. Every day seems like a whirlwind.

There's no break, and no rest. The thought of adding yet another responsibility to your list of things to do might seem crazy. But if it's getting more patients into the door so that you can help them, is it worth it?

BONUS: Do you see what I did there? I wrote down the 5 most common questions I receive about blogging, and I wrote a few paragraphs on them. At the time of publishing this book, ironically, my Website for the Web-design business will just have been created (sitesforcare.com). It's long overdue — I've just been too busy with other people's sites. But you can bet that when I do put the site up I will already have 5 weeks worth of content in this tip alone, and it took me all of 15 minutes to write.

You can schedule blog posts, by the way. So instead of writing once a week, you could write once a month and just write 4 posts that you schedule out. Or you could write once a quarter and schedule out 16 posts (although I would recommend monthly if you're going to schedule stuff so quality doesn't diminish). Just be sure that your posts are going out every week at the same day. You want to train your readers to know when to check back on your site. It also helps ward off procrastination as you build the habit to do the same thing at the same time each week.

There's also no shame at all in hiring a copywriter to write your blog for you. There are different ways to set this up, but the most hands-off way is that the copywriter will research what is going on in your industry and then write an article based off his/her research and post it into the blog on your behalf. Another way would be that he/she would interview your staff on certain questions and then take your answers and re-write them in a way that sounds good. If you need introduced to a copywriter who is familiar with the health-care field, I would be happy to do so. Just let me know.

14. DON'T Use Social Media "Just Because"

Social media is one of those buzz words. For the most part, we're all on it (although personally I only post, I don't read anyone else's stuff. Too much of a time-suck and heart-risk), but you need to think long and hard about who your target audience is and if they are making health care decisions based on social media. I am by no means a social media expert, so feel free to ignore my advice. But if you were to do social media, I believe there's a very effective way of getting people to your site: fear-inspiring headlines. Now some of this depends on what you feel comfortable with. Some don't feel comfortable writing a sensationalized headline like "Could You Be at Risk of a Heart Attack As You Read This Sentence?" Personally, I believe that if you can help someone and potentially save their life by providing a sensationalized headline to get them to click and to bring a serious problem to their attention, then the ends justify the means. These kinds of posts are very viral in nature (no pun intended for viral diseases), especially if you follow the post with "Share With Your Loved Ones." Is it shameless self-promotion? Yes. But like I said, I believe that if the article is truthful and you can book an appointment that potentially saves someone's life, then it is worth it. But ask yourself if social media is the right place for you to be, or if your time could better be spent somewhere else. You can also go half-way with it. You don't need to post every single day, for example. You could just post when you have a new blog. Or you could share a news story. The point of social media is to build relationships and give people vital information that they need. If this is a task you feel you're up to, then by all means be there. But don't make it your whole strategy like is popular these days.

15. DO Make it Mobile-Friendly with "Responsive Design"

Back in the dawn of mobile browsing (which seems like it was just yesterday) when both Websites and mobile browsers were less sophisticated, you needed an entirely different site to display to your mobile friends. Websites would check what kind of device the visitor was on, and if they were on a mobile device, they would be sent to a mobile-specific site (like m.Facebook.com, or m.Google.com).

These days, both mobile and tablet devices along with the Websites they browse on have become much smarter through something called "responsive design." Responsive design means that you have one Website design that is actively checking for the screen size. If the screen drops below a certain size, it automatically resizes everything and shifts things around to make it easier to browse on smaller devices. You can sometimes even test this in your computer's browser by just making the browser window smaller. On a responsive Website you will see items start to shift and move as you squeeze them into a smaller box. On a non-responsive site things will stay the same size and get cut off.

In 2015 there was a big scare with "Mobilegeddon" which was a change in Google's search algorithm that checked if a Website was mobile-friendly up to their high standards, and that if the site was *not*, it would be cut out of mobile search results completely.

The bottom line is that at the time of writing this book, 58% of device time is spent on a mobile device, *not* a laptop or PC, and that number is on a consistent rise. This means that if your site is *not* mobile friendly, you are missing out on a huge chunk of your traffic who come to your site and leave due to it not being usable.

16. DON'T Use a Large Homepage Slider

This is a usually losing battle I have with many folks. I mentioned earlier the "fold", and that having the most important information above the fold so that users don't have to scroll down to get it is vital. Sliders take up most of that fold, especially on small screens. They also make the site slower to load, and they usually transition much too fast to get any actual information from them. Instead, I recommend putting an attention-grabbing headline on the home page, maybe a video, and some kind of call to action or lead-generator.

It's become fashionable to create sites that look like the one in the example, with gigantic sliders that take up almost the entire fold. There are even Web design tricks that you can use to make the slider full-screen until someone scrolls. Sometimes these sliders display images, other times they display videos or dynamic interactive content. I will admit, it's really cool. It's beautiful, it's fun, and when I see it I think "ooooo…cool!". But I can tell you right now that split testing shows over and over again that sliders are bad for usability, conversion, and even SEO. Some of my clients insist on them, and despite my efforts to the contrary, I implement them. But I can tell you right now that it is a mistake.

Don't do it.

Large homepage sliders (or any sliders at all) are typically a waste of valuable above-fold space. What purpose do they serve?

17. DO Track Your Results

There's this excellent tool called Google Analytics that is an extremely powerful way to track visitors on your Website. Better yet, it's free. Not only does it tell you *how many* visitors you get every hour of every day, but it tells you how you're getting them, where they're located, what pages they visited on your site, how long they stayed on each of those pages, where they left your site, what links they clicked on, and so on. There's so much information in Google Analytics that I by no means consider myself even close to an expert on it. That being said, there are some important metrics that I like to look at and cross-reference with some other data that we're collecting on your site.

I'm going to explain each of these pieces of data with the following example: *Yesterday, you visited Facebook for 5 minutes. You clicked on 3 people's pages and then got off after you saw a drama-provoking post by your Aunt on her page.*

Sessions: This is the number of times in the selected span of time that people have *started* a visit on your Website. Your entire Facebook visit in the example above counts as one session, even though you visited multiple pages. If you would close out of Facebook completely and come back that would count as 2 sessions.

Page Views: This is the number of pages that people have visited, overall. In the example above, you had a total of 4 page views (1 for the homepage, 3 for the people's pages you clicked on).

Users: This is the number of individuals who visited the site over the specified span of time. You count as one user, no matter how many times you come back to Facebook.

Pages / Session: Pretty self-explanatory. This is how many pages on average people visit during each session. If you visited Facebook and did the exact same thing every time, your average pages/session would be 4. For the sites I design the average is around 2.5 because we get people information quickly and book an appointment. If you have high pages/session it means one of two things: either you have lots of fantastic content that people are reading and enjoying, or your site is difficult to navigate so people are having a hard time finding what they want.

Average Session Duration: Again, this is a simple one. This is how long sessions last on average. These numbers can be slightly skewed depending on your bounce rate (below), because bounced visitors aren't always counted toward the site duration. In the example above, your session lasted 5 minutes on Facebook. While we don't know the average duration per session for Facebook specifically, we do know that the average time spent daily is 21 minutes (which factors into 5 whole days and some change each and every year — one reason I stopped visiting).

Bounce Rate: The overall site bounce rate is the percentage of visitors who come to the site, visit one page, and leave without visiting any other pages. Most think of this as a bad thing, but it can be misleading. For example, it could be that people are coming to your site to get one piece of information like a phone number or to fill out a contact form. In this case they're getting the information they were looking for and leaving the site, contributing to a high bounce rate.

% of New Sessions: This is the percentage of sessions that were undergone by visitors who haven't been to your site before. The opposite of this percentage is the number of *repeat* visitors you received.

Acquisition: This is where you received your visitors from, whether it be a search engine, from social media, or from someone just typing your Website into the address bar.

Behavior: This is one of my favorites. This shows you a breakdown of every page on your site and gives you the statistics above for each of them. You can figure out what your most popular pages are and also where people might be getting confused (if they leave the site without doing anything else).

Jotform Submissions: Jotform is the tool that I use to create appointment forms on the Websites I design. I like to take the total number of form submissions over a period of time and divide it by the number of visitors received to get a "site conversion rate". For example, if you received 3,000 visitors last month and had 30 people fill out the form, that means that 1% (which, believe it or not, is actually a fine conversion rate for most Websites) of people who come to your Website are booking an appointment. So you know that each time you get 100 people to your Website you're going to, on average, book at least one appointment.

Patients Converted: The last number I like to look at is out of the number of those forms submitted, how many of those patients showed up for appointments and actually become long-term patients? Let's say that out of the 30 who filled out the form last month, 25 came in for an appointment and became new patients. That gives you a patient conversion rate of 83%. If you do the math (83% of 1%) you'll know that, on average, you will get one new patient for every 116 visitors to your site. Yes, it takes a little math, but it's worth doing to know your numbers.

18. DON'T Track Your Results Too Little, Too Late

Here's a short tip: don't track your results once a year, or once a quarter. One client who I do some consulting work for had a previous vendor charging them tons of money a month for quarterly analytics reports (something that the client could have gotten themselves whenever they wanted), and checking that infrequently is pointless. I would recommend checking the above important statistics at least once a month, at the same time each month, and keeping a spreadsheet so that you can easily compare other months. Then you should actually figure out what the numbers *mean*. If you saw an increase in conversions, why was that? Were you blogging more? Did you change something on the appointment booking form? What about if conversions dropped? Why would that be? Could it be the time of year? The great thing is that if you do this long enough you can start seeing big patterns in times of year and the number of patients who visit the Website or book appointments and you can prepare accordingly.

19. DO Use Testimonials

Testimonials are <u>by far</u> the <u>easiest</u> way to build trust between yourself and potential patients whom you have never met before. They're social proof. They tell your visitor: *Others have been in my situation before, and I can trust that I am in safe hands with XYZ.*

Where should testimonials be displayed? Everywhere. On the homepage, on the "About" page, on the "Contact" page, and any other page where you feel that people may need a little reassurance. Earlier, I mentioned that you can have a perfect site with just 5 pages. If you were to add a 6th page, I would make it a "Success Stories" page. The great thing is that in most traditional businesses, in order for testimonials to be as effective as possible, you have to have full names along with pictures of the person giving the testimonial. The ultimate is to have a video testimonial.

But in the health care business this isn't the case. You can totally (and should, for HIPAA), get away with just having a testimonial that is attributed to "JS, Pittsburgh" or "MB, Aspinwall, PA", and no one is going to think twice. If you aren't already, you should be encouraging every single patient who comes into your office to leave you comments. Whether you collect these through a system like Press

Ganey, or you just have patients write their comments on a card that they deposit in a box with permission to use their comments on the site, it is a *must* for building trust. I had one doctor who was helping me on a Website say that he *hated* testimonials and didn't want them on his site. This was one thing I wouldn't budge on, because he had dozens of *fantastic* comments from patients that we could feature. We ended up compromising on a small text-slider on the homepage that cycled through all of the great reviews. I attribute their high conversion rates in large part to these testimonials being there, although I have no scientific evidence of the fact.

The bottom line is that if you have them you should use them, and that if you don't have them you should get them.

20. DO Use Photos and Videos

Flip through any magazine and you'll notice that you're actively searching for two things: Headlines, and usually more-so, images. Images are so important on your Website. They serve several purposes:

1. Break up text and keep the visitor from getting bored or tired.

2. Help explain that which is hard to explain with text alone. "A picture is worth a thousand words."

3. Help familiarize the visitor with you, your staff, and your locations.

Videos are equally important for the same reasons, but they're truly great because they allow your visitors to get to know your personality. They also give a lot of information without taking up a lot of space. It's for this reason that I recommend putting a video on the homepage. It doesn't take up too much of "the fold" and it allows you to get your primary message out there. As I said earlier, I don't recommend auto-playing videos. Testing shows that they more often than not get an annoyed visitor to leave than they do keep their attention. There are some exceptions to this, one of them being that sometimes on thank-you pages I like to have an auto-played video that tells people what to expect next. For example, the video might say something like "thanks for filling out our form. You can expect to be contacted via phone within the next few hours. In the meantime, check out the links below. If you'd like to save some time in the waiting room, print and fill out the new patient form and bring it with you to your visit..." At this point, they've already given their information, so the worst case-scenario if you autoplay the video is that they leave that page but you already have their information to follow up with them.

21. DON'T Use Your iPhone

When it comes to photos and video, one tendency might be to try to capture these things with an iPhone or similar device. These devices take *stunning* photos — they really do. For small images of the location, an iPhone may be suitable. For larger photos or photos of people it isn't so much that the iPhone isn't a sufficient camera — it's more of a lighting issue. So having professional-grade lighting there is definitely worth it. For video, I would not recommend doing any less than working with a professional. You're not going to be able to get anywhere near the quality of video with an iPhone or even a D-SLR camera that you would with a professional videographer's lighting, cameras, microphones, and expertise in scripting and directing. I work with an excellent videographer who does amazing work directing, filming, and editing videos for health care sites. Again, I would be happy to make an introduction.

Typically, I include photography and videography in my packages to make it really affordable for my clients. This way, they can get amazing quality media on their Website without paying a fortune and without the hassles that can go along with finding and hiring a photographer and videographer.

22. DON'T Rely Completely on a Designer

This is a hard one for me to write. Part of me deep down wants to say, "No. You *need* to rely on your designer!" because that's what's going to make me the most money. But truthfully, I know that with the way the Web works now, you don't need a designer to make most minor changes. You certainly don't need a designer to be the one to add content to your site like blog posts, because that's what we're using a CMS (Content Management System) for. I can't tell you how other Web designers work, because I haven't worked with them, but I can tell you how I typically do things. I offer 3 packages when I meet with clients. The first two packages include a Website training and unlimited Email support. What this means is that I train everyone on staff who wants to be trained in a single training session where I teach them as much as I can in regards to how to edit the Website and add content. I explain the CMS I use (Wordpress), and I answer any questions they may have. My goal is for my clients to all be self-sufficient from the blogging and content-creation end of things. Email support means that at any time, my clients can ask me questions via Email on how to do things. I will explain, also via Email, how they should go about doing what they're trying to do as best as I can. Sometimes I will even include video tutorials that lay out, step by step, the actions they need to take. If they decide that it's over their head and they want me to make the change myself, then they'll be billed at an hourly rate for me to make those changes. This is how I'm able to keep my standard prices low — because I offer Email support with an hourly rate model.

Another option for my clients who know they don't have the time to modify their site and they just want me to make changes and improvements as we go along is to pay monthly for a certain number of hours per month. For these clients, I am constantly making changes, suggesting improvements to the site, etc. My goal is to use up the hours every month doing great work so that they don't waste them.

Neither way is right or wrong, it just depends on what the client's needs are. Some want someone on staff to be the dedicated point person who will make the changes, and others just want me to make changes for them. The important thing is that either way the changes are being made. Unfortunately, some put a point person in charge but nothing ever gets done because they don't take action on the suggestions I make.

23. DO Use a Lead Generator

At last…the tip I keep mentioning!

This is one of the most important tips in this book because it relates to all of the visitors who come to your site and leave without booking an appointment.

There are some people who come to your site, look around, and then just disappear. You'll have no idea why, but it will be very, very frustrating.

This is where what we call "Direct Response Marketing" comes in. This is how we increase the number of people who come to our site and actually fill out our form.

Like I mentioned earlier, Web site traffic is a numbers game, but it may not be the numbers you think. For example, would you rather get 1000 people to your site each day with your SEO strategy and only convert 10 of them, or would you rather get 100 people to your site each day and convert 20 of them? Obviously it makes more sense to focus on getting the people who *are* visiting your site to buy something than it does to just bring more non-paying visitors to your site. This shift in mentality alone can completely change your Website success.

So what is Direct Response Marketing? Direct Response Marketing is all about getting people to take some kind of action. It's not enough to just get people to your site, and it's not enough to get people to hear your brand name — you need to get them to do something, whether that is coming in for an appointment or giving their Email address or whatever.

There are two types of sales on a Website, by the way — there's a one-step sale and a two-step sale. I know we don't like to think of new patients in a health care practice as "sales," but that's what they are when you get right down to it.

Now, in a one-step sale you are asking your visitors to fill out an appointment form right now so they can come into the office. This can be done, but it also helps to have the next option, which is a two-step sale. In a two-step sale you are giving your visitors some kind of value in exchange for their information and permission to follow up with them.

An example of a two-step sale for health care would be that instead of trying to get everybody to book an appointment right off the bat, you offer something like a free report titled "The 7 Secrets to a Healthier and Happier Life" that the visitor can get for free by submitting their name and Email. This is the first step. The second step is where you're going to follow up with them and urge them to book an appointment to come into the office.

Here are some statistics for you: 3% of everyone who visits your site are active-searching prospective patients. These are the people who are actively searching for a health care provider and are going to choose one very, very soon. 7% of the people who visit your site have that need, but aren't really searching for options too seriously. They are on the fence, though, and may become 3% given the right message. 30% have a need, but it's not great enough to act on right now. There is no way they are going to book an appointment right now, but they may want to make an appointment in the future. 30% do not have a need at all, and will likely never be patients. Another 30% are simply not interested in *your* organization. Basically, these people are never going to choose you for whatever reason, and there's no way you're going to pull them to your side.

So out of all of these, only 3% are ready to book an

appointment. It's that 37% of people who have a need but aren't going to book right now that need the 2-step sale. They're in the research phase, gaining more information so that they can make an informed buying decision when the time comes.

So you offer these visitors something in exchange for their information. This way you can continue to follow up with them. Once the day comes that they become 3-percenters, you will be top of mind because you've been following up with them this whole time.

The easiest and quickest way to do this is to write a short report or have one written — only a few pages long — based on some piece of vital information that your prospects are already asking for. You offer this report in exchange for their Names and Email addresses, and you deliver it via Email after they give this information.

So this is the other half of the Website equation. One half is building the Website and actually getting people there, but the other (arguably more important) half is having a system in place that takes visitors from knowing nothing about you, to educating them, to following up with them, and finally to them becoming paying customers.

This doesn't need to happen overnight, by the way. If you want to create a report to give away I would start with that. If you're a natural writer like myself, this will be easy for you. Some others prefer to talk. If that's the case, you might want to give away a free interview that you record with a friend or colleague that gives people information they're looking for. You could also record yourself "speaking" the report and then have someone transcribe it for $5 on fiverr.com. Then you need some way of capturing those leads. I like to put the free gift on every page with a small form below it that I create using Jotform (mentioned earlier) to encourage people to sign up. After all, we only have 2.5 pages to get them to take some kind of action, whether that be to fill out some kind of booking form or it's to get the free gift.

24. DO Have a Follow Up System in Place

Now that you've captured a lead you can either manually follow-up with them, or you can use "marketing automation" software which does things for you automatically.

What I love about using marketing automation software is that when someone fills out a form to get one of my free gifts, they automatically receive an Email with the gift. Then, in a day, they receive another Email making sure they received it and asking if they have any questions. They continue to receive these Emails until they take further action, where they're put into another sequence. I can do this process for hundreds of people at once without spending any time or even thinking about it happening. That's the true power of marketing automation.

In any case, whether you're using marketing automation or doing things manually, it's extremely important that you have a follow up *system* in place. You should sit down and ask yourself: what do you want your potential patient to experience, from the time they first visit your Website, to their first appointment, to what happens after, etc. Write it down *exactly* as a step-by-step system and then figure out how to make that system happen.

This should be a step-by-step guide that is so easy than anyone
could follow it. The benefit of making things automatic using
marketing-automation is that you'll be a lot less likely to be
complacent. For the online Email-related steps, they will be sent
out automatically, and for the offline steps you can have the
automation software send you a reminder to do them. It takes the
thinking out of having a consistent follow-up process, which is a
good thing.

Take this quote from direct response marketing guru Dan
Kennedy, from his book *No BS Ruthless Management of People and
Profits*, "…One of these far more valuable assets is systems and
procedures, coupled with enforcement."

"McDonald's® is able to deliver millions of products to
millions of customers day in, day out, in outlets scattered all over
the country, owned by independent operators, without poisoning
a lot of people, with consistent (albeit mediocre, but satisfactory)
quality, at value prices, and dominate its field — all with pimply
faced, hormones-raging, MTV-attention-deficient teenagers
NOT because of visionary leadership, charismatic leaders, and
motivational speakers, or happy-talk team-building campouts.

This improbable achievement occurs because of systems."

While I get that you aren't McDonalds and that health care seems almost the antithesis of the leading fast-food chain, the point is made: systems are vital to delivering a consistent experience every time. They're also vital to converting that 37% I talked about into patients.

25. DO Use a Newsletter to Stay Top of Mind

How do you follow up with those who come to your site and take your "lead generator," leaving their information behind? The answer is simple: take the blogs that you *should* be writing every week and use a system like Mailchimp, AWeber, or ActiveCampaign (the latter doubling as super-affordable Marketing Automation software) to send a weekly Email newsletter to these people.

I would also *highly* recommend that you send a physical newsletter as well, *at least* once a month, *at least* to your best patients. A friend of mine who helps write such newsletters wrote one for a dentist she worked with. The dentist didn't do a ton with it, but he *did* put it out in the waiting area for people to read. An orthodontist came into the office, saw it, and loved it so much that they wanted to use it in their office. The dentist makes a nice side-business now just selling his newsletter to other health-care providers to keep in their offices.

I implemented both online and offline newsletters for my magic business, and it's no wonder I get so many people who hire me for every event that they host. I'm constantly in their digital and physical mailboxes, reminding them.

Your newsletters don't even *have* to be all health-related. While you can certainly include a tip or two, I've actually found more success just sharing fun and personal stories. One of my highest opened and responded-to Email campaigns of late was the one where I talked about getting a new dog. No mention of magic or events. Did one of the docs get a new dog? Did the office manager have a baby? Did you host a holiday party? Write about it! You'd be surprised at the responses you get from your patients when you share something a little personal.

26. DO Invest In An Experienced Copywriter if You Aren't Willing to Be One Yourself

I firmly believe that no one knows your patients and your office as much as you, so you are the best person to talk about those things. That being said, I understand that not everyone likes to write, and not everyone is *good* at writing. One option for such folks is to invest in a copywriter — someone who writes for a living — to write for you. They can write your blog posts, your marketing materials, the pages on your Website, your newsletter, your lead generator, and anything else you want them to write.

As I described before, typically the process involves them interviewing your office and then doing some independent research themselves into what is hot in your field. Then they'll write based on that. The copywriter I work with and recommend is much more strategic. For example, I recently had an orthopedic office who I am consulting with ask for a copywriter to write their blog. He had a meeting with them and determined that while the blog was important, it wasn't their biggest need, copy-writing wise. What they needed were some new staff in key positions.

So he wrote up some recruitment Emails for them and they got responses from A-Lister recruits within a few hours. So being with someone who not only writes great copy, but someone who understands and is in-tune with your needs is very important as well.

27. DO Take the Next Step

I tried to make this book as easy to read as possible. Hopefully you found that I've accomplished this goal and you were able to extract some valuable information.

I'm a big reader, myself. I *try* to read about a book a week, which may or may not happen depending on the week. Usually these are non-fiction books on marketing and business, but I enjoy the occasional fiction or philosophical book from time to time as well.

What I've realized while reading all of these books full of great lessons and advice is that they're worthless if I don't *implement*. I have no idea where you are in your Web design process. It could be that you don't have a Website yet, and it could be that you've had a Website for years. That's why I wrote this book to cover a wide variety of tips for both the new and experienced alike.

If there is any way I can help you, I would love to do so. Please Email me at me@collinstover.com. Additionally, you can get free weekly tips just like these that are related to implementing the perfect health-care Website by visiting www.Sitesforcare.com.

THE MOST INCREDIBLE FREE GIFT (WORTH $97.47):

To get a jump-start on your Website, visit
sitesforcare.com/book-gift right now for a free audio
version of this book, templates, checklists, and other
free resources.

www.sitesforcare.com/book-gift